DATE DUE

OCT 05 '12			

Smell

Text: Andreu Llamas
Illustrations: Francisco Arredondo

El olfato © Copyright EDICIONES ESTE, S. A., 1995,
Barcelona, Spain

Smell Copyright © 1996 by Chelsea House Publishers, a
division of Main Line Book Co. All rights reserved.

1 3 5 7 9 8 6 4 2

Library of Congress Cataloging-in-Publication Data

Llamas, Andreu.
  [Olfato. English]
  Smell / [text, Andreu Llamas ; illustrations, Francisco
    Arredondo]. p. cm. — (Five senses of the animal world)
  Includes index.
  Summary: Discusses the sense which enables some animals
to detect their prey, search for food, signal danger, or find their
way back to where they had been long ago.
  ISBN 0-7910-3492-5. — ISBN 0-7910-3498-4 (pbk.)
  1. Smell—Juvenile literature. [1. Smell. 2. Senses and sensa-
tion. 3. Animals—Physiology.] I. Arredondo, Francisco, ill. II.
Title. III. Series.
QP458.L5613   1996   95-17488
591.1'826—dc20   CIP
                                                    AC

Contents

Smell

CHELSEA HOUSE PUBLISHERS

New York • Philadelphia

How Do We Smell?

Smell is the sense that enables animals to recognize and differentiate between chemical substances in their surroundings.

This sense is very acute in some animals, such as dogs, and is very important for survival.

The sensitive organ for smell is inside the nostrils. Nostrils are part of the respiratory tract and are completely covered in a sensitive mucosa, called pituitary. This mucosa also maintains the necessary heat and humidity we need to condition the air we breathe, even when it is too hot or too cold.

The smelling cells are in the upper part of the nostrils in the pituitary area on top of the ethmoid bone. These cells are very sensitive to the volatile cells suspended in the air.

The signals are sent to the brain, where they are translated. The brain interprets these smells using a particular memory; the brain keeps a memory of smells that relates it with when it was last smelled.

The brain is also able to get used to continual exposure to one smell, even if it is very foul. In such a case, the animal or person becomes accustomed to it and no longer detects it.

A dog's sense of smell is highly developed; scientists have calculated that its nose is a million times more sensitive than a human's.

It is difficult to appreciate the importance of smell for other animals. A bison, for instance, is able to detect a pond more than 6 miles (9 kilometers) away!

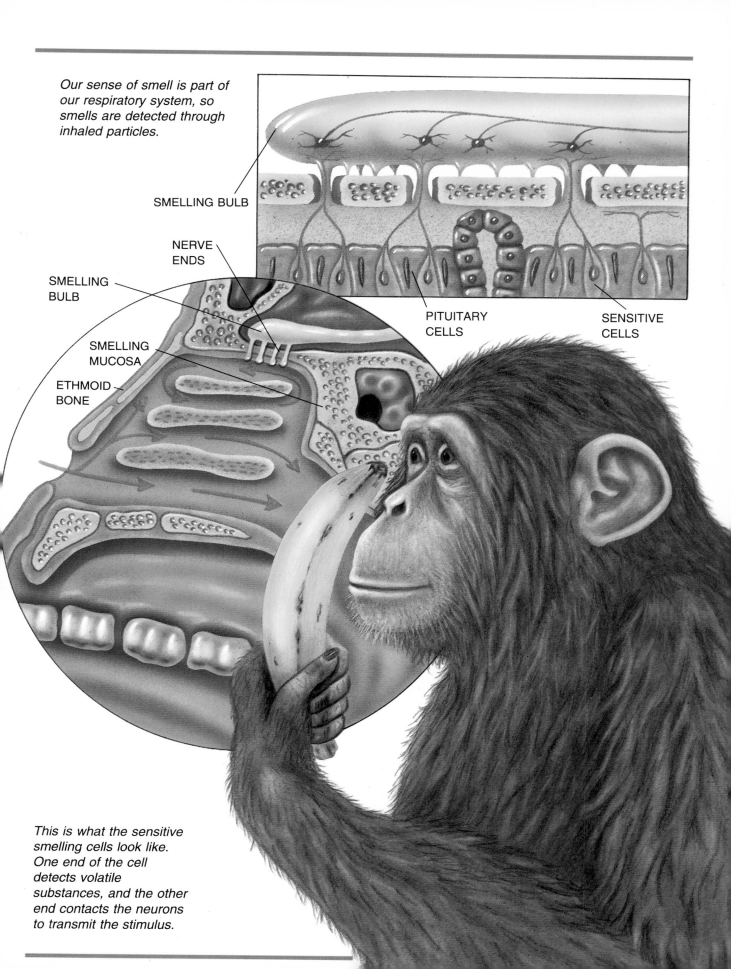

Our sense of smell is part of our respiratory system, so smells are detected through inhaled particles.

SMELLING BULB

NERVE ENDS

SMELLING BULB

SMELLING MUCOSA

ETHMOID BONE

PITUITARY CELLS

SENSITIVE CELLS

This is what the sensitive smelling cells look like. One end of the cell detects volatile substances, and the other end contacts the neurons to transmit the stimulus.

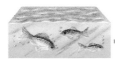

Smelling Underwater

Can you smell under the water? In the water, the difference between taste and smell is not as distinct as in the air.

In the water, the sense of smell can give chemical information of the presence of a predator or prey in the distance. Taste informs about objects in the mouth.

For a fish to smell, the water carrying the chemical substances must come into contact with the tissue on the fish where the receptors are. The water circulates through the smelling sack by means of different systems. Some fish have *cilia*, which drive the water through their movement; in other species, the water circulates simply through the swimming motion; and there are other fish that bring in the water with breathing movements. Smells have already been dissolved underwater, and some fish are able to follow a scent. Fish have a highly developed sense of smell and the parts of the brain devoted to this sense are very large.

Smell has many applications in fish: it can detect predators or prey or be used for chemical communication between members of the same species. In many fish, the sense of smell is also important for social behavior.

Land vertebrates that have adapted to sea life have a very poor sense of smell. *Cetaceans* have lost most of their ability to smell in the open air and have very weak receptors. They probably lost this sense when their nostrils moved to the top of their heads to form the *spiracle*. These nostrils close underwater and only open when the animal is on the surface.

Starfish give off a characteristic smell. When they approach, cockles smell their presence and can escape.

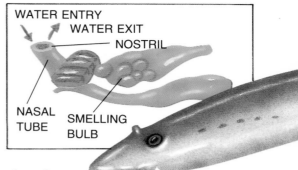

Agnatha
(fish without jaws) only have one single nostril and a smelling sack with many folds that cover the sensitive tissue.

WATER ENTRY — WATER EXIT — NOSTRIL — NASAL TUBE — SMELLING BULB

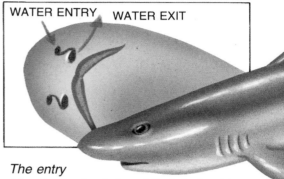

The entry
of water in sharks' nostrils is helped by external structures.

WATER ENTRY — WATER EXIT

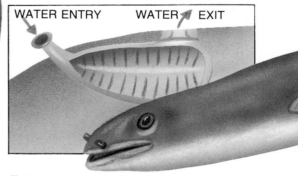

Eels sense smells thanks to a ciliate nasal capsule.

Most fish, such as this grouper, have two nostrils on each side of their heads.

WATER ENTRY — WATER EXIT

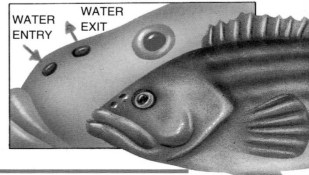

WATER ENTRY — WATER EXIT

Not all animals can use their sense of smell underwater. Cetaceans keep their nostrils closed when they submerge, so they cannot detect smells.

A Salmon's Guidance

How does a salmon find its way back to the waters where it was born years before?

As well as being important for detecting food, the sense of smell is fundamental for guidance during some species' *migrations*, when they travel enormous distances to return to the place where they were born, such as the salmon.

Salmon are born in rivers and afterward go toward the sea. They spend the next five years of their lives in the sea, and then, when they need to reproduce, return to the same river where they were born five years before.

This return journey may be as much as 800 miles, so how do they remember the correct route? Salmon find the river where they were born thanks to their sense of smell—they literally smell their way home. Salmon always find the river mouth and then swim upstream against the current, always going the correct way at any deviation or stream.

The sense of smell is highly developed in fish and they are also able to maintain the ability to distinguish between different smells for a long time. Scientists have discovered that young fish remember smells better than old fish.

Of all fish migrations, eels stand out. North American and European freshwater eels are born in the Sargasso Sea and travel for years until they reach the rivers where they will grow—a journey of more than 4,340 miles! When they reproduce, the eels make the long journey back to the Sargasso Sea.

The sea turtle returns to the same beach where it was born 10 years earlier to spawn. On its long, 1,240-mile (2,000-kilometer) journey, it is guided by smell and magnetism.

Salmon are very headstrong and try again and again to overcome the waterfalls until they reach their birthplace to reproduce. During their journey, they never make a mistake when they have to take a deviation in the river.

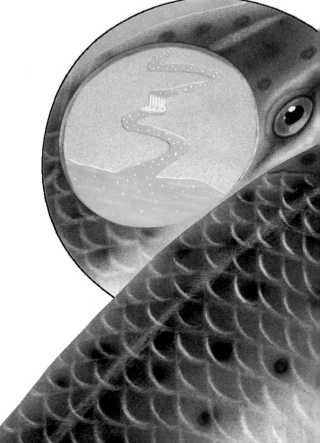

When the red barbel is attacked, it begins to secrete substances (pheromones) that sound the alarm for the rest of the group.

The Smelling World of Insects

For many insects, the most important information they receive does not come from their sight, but rather from their senses of smell and taste.

Ants, for example, constantly leave a trail of chemical information and always touch each other to transmit the smell of the nest.

There are some insects that are incredibly sensitive to the calling of sexual scents. The butterfly of the female silkworm sends out a pheromone, which it spreads through the air over great distances, and males can detect it from as far away as 7 miles (12 kilometers), thanks to their complex antennae. When the female is ready to mate, she begins to flap her wings to spread the scent produced by special glands she has on her abdomen. The scent travels in the air in tiny concentrations until some particles reach the antennae of a male. The insect analyzes and studies all the smells that reach it and immediately goes to look for the source of the scent of the female.

Often, when insects fly in a seemingly indecisive way, what they are really doing is sweeping the air with their antennae in order to detect some molecules of the smells that interest them, such as food or females. It seems impossible that the small surface of the antennae can pick up such small scent concentrations, but they can. After going around to find where the irresistible scent is coming from, the insect goes off unhesitatingly in the right direction.

Ball beetles appear a few moments after an excrement has been made because they have to compete to get the best part. They are able to find fresh manure within 60 seconds after it is left.

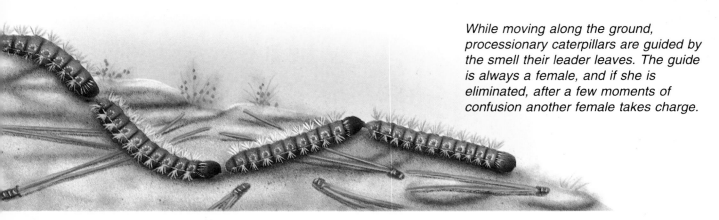

While moving along the ground, processionary caterpillars are guided by the smell their leader leaves. The guide is always a female, and if she is eliminated, after a few moments of confusion another female takes charge.

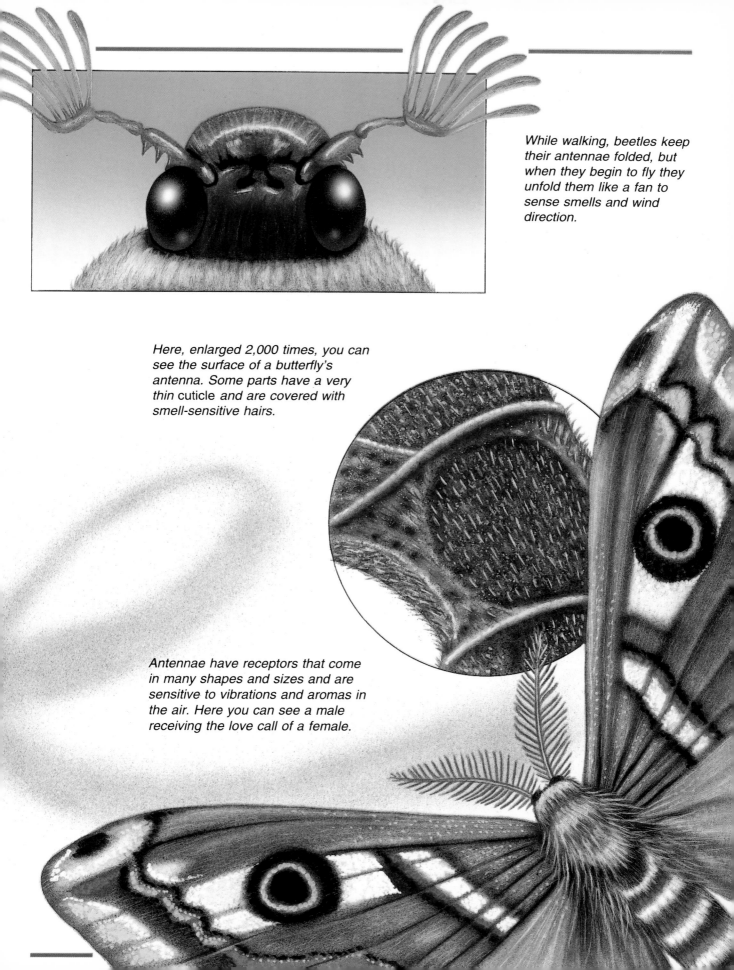

While walking, beetles keep their antennae folded, but when they begin to fly they unfold them like a fan to sense smells and wind direction.

Here, enlarged 2,000 times, you can see the surface of a butterfly's antenna. Some parts have a very thin cuticle and are covered with smell-sensitive hairs.

Antennae have receptors that come in many shapes and sizes and are sensitive to vibrations and aromas in the air. Here you can see a male receiving the love call of a female.

An Insect's Chemical Weapons

Insects can use smells for many different functions. For example, there are many social insects that are able to generate chemical alarms to which the whole colony reacts at once.

In most species of ant, the main signal of alert and danger consists of a chemical secretion that contains various components, especially formic acid, which enables it to give stronger stimuli as the danger increases. The scent language of ants is very rich and their different "words" are produced in special glands. When the nest is in danger, ants fire an acid secretion at the intruder. The smell of this acid causes the ants outside the nest to run away; for those that are inside the nest, the smell represents the order to attack the enemy.

Many insects use repellent substances. Some beetles launch a spray of formic acid, which burns the skin and damages the sight of predators. There are also insects that have learned to use the smell languages of other species. For instance, there are many beetles that live near ants either as predators or parasites or get food from them without harming them; in order to be welcome, they imitate the chemical smells and the behavior of the ants. Some beetles' *larvae* give off a pheromone that is attractive to ants, which adopt them and put them in their incubation chambers to nurse them. Some species, such as Leptothorax, avoid attracting aggressive ants by ceasing to give off scents.

There are spiders that hang a sticky ball at the end of their web that copies the sexual aroma of a female night butterfly. When a male attracted by the scent approaches, the spider eats it before it even realizes it has been tricked.

The bomber beetle defends itself from predators by spraying them with chemical substances, which cause blisters on the skin. It can even make toads retreat.

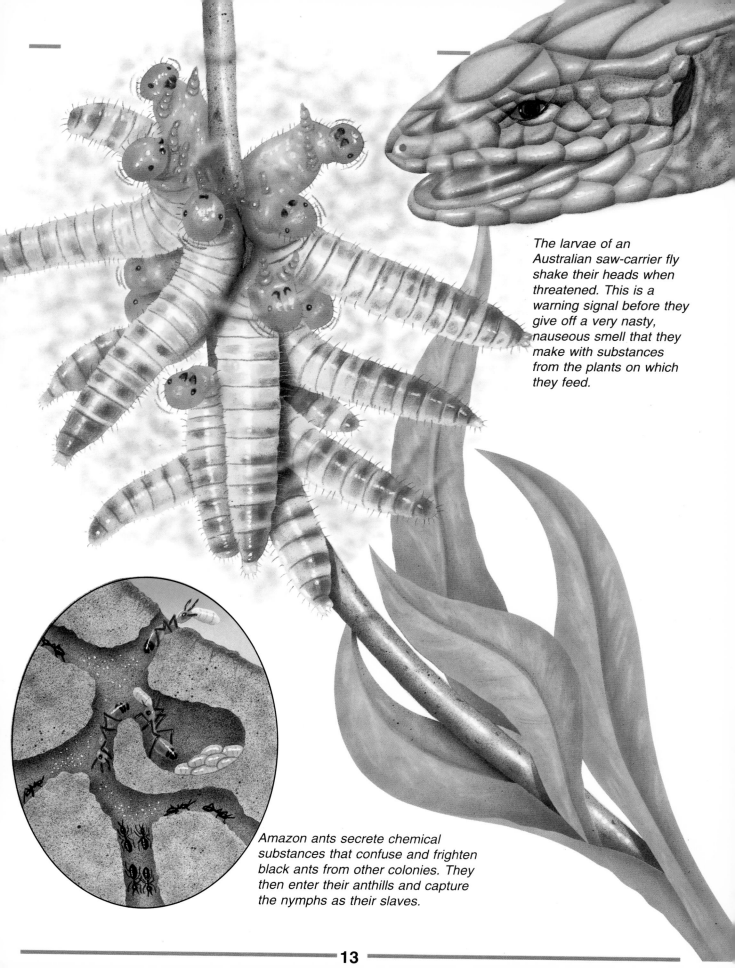

The larvae of an Australian saw-carrier fly shake their heads when threatened. This is a warning signal before they give off a very nasty, nauseous smell that they make with substances from the plants on which they feed.

Amazon ants secrete chemical substances that confuse and frighten black ants from other colonies. They then enter their anthills and capture the nymphs as their slaves.

A Shark's Sense of Smell

Smell is one of the main ways a shark detects its prey.

These terrible predators have their sense of smell in the smelling sacks of their snouts. Inside, they have membranes that are very sensitive to substances dissolved in the water and this is why they can detect the blood of a wounded prey from a great distance.

As an aid while hunting, sharks are more sensitive to the smell of certain substances, such as some fish skin components and blood.

Sharks usually swim in circles while checking the smell and the taste of the water. The first information a shark receives about the presence of a possible prey are vibrations, but then it uses its sense of smell to get more exact information.

When a shark detects a chemical stimulus that attracts it, it can follow the "trail" it has discovered by swimming against the current carrying the scent, or it can zigzag across the trail time after time.

Sharks are so sensitive to some smells, such as blood, that the animals' behavior is affected even with very small concentrations. As the shark closes in on the source of the scent, it detects higher and higher concentrations and can react by biting any visible object close at hand.

Sharks' nasal sacks allow them to detect very small concentrations of chemical substances.

Here you can see what the smelling tissue of a shark looks like under a microscope.

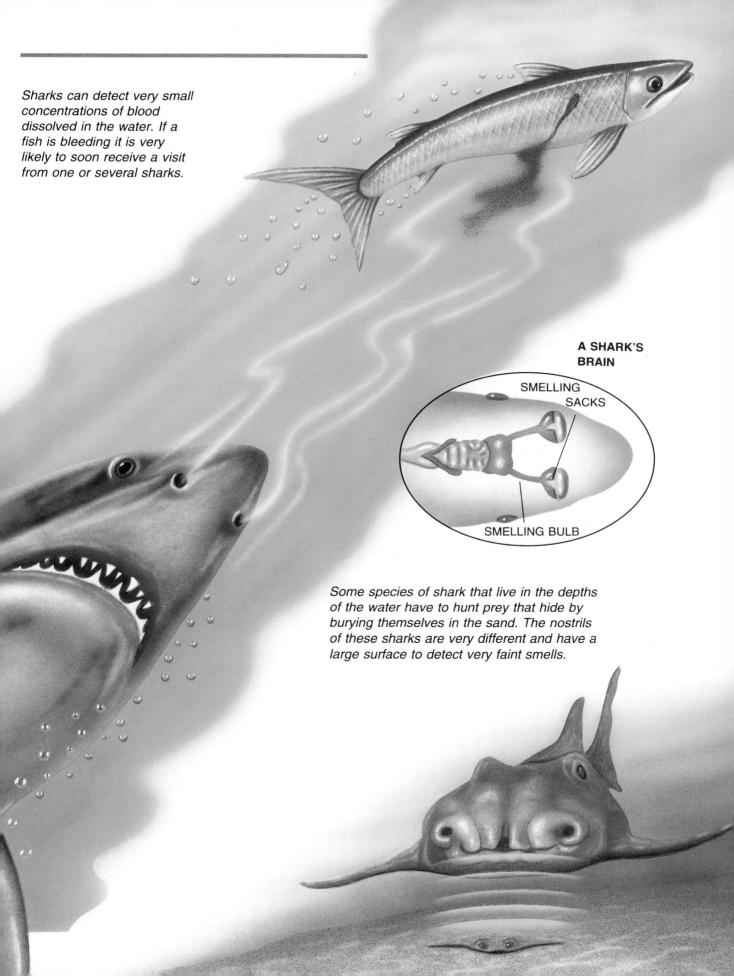

Sharks can detect very small concentrations of blood dissolved in the water. If a fish is bleeding it is very likely to soon receive a visit from one or several sharks.

A SHARK'S BRAIN

SMELLING SACKS

SMELLING BULB

Some species of shark that live in the depths of the water have to hunt prey that hide by burying themselves in the sand. The nostrils of these sharks are very different and have a large surface to detect very faint smells.

Smelling with the Tongue

Have you ever wondered why snakes constantly stick out their tongues?

Many reptiles are active carnivores and hunters that look for and capture their prey thanks to the help of their sense of smell. You surely have observed a snake while it moves; it continually pokes out its long *bifid* tongue. What it is doing is detecting smells that give it information.

The bifid tongue of lizards and snakes returns to the mouth after collecting the scent particles on the ground. Inside their mouths, these animals have two small grooves on their palates that make up Jacobson's organ and are covered in a smelling tissue. When a snake's tongue enters its mouth, the two ends run along the grooves in Jacobson's organ, which make a detailed analysis of the chemical composition of the particles collected.

These reptiles' sense of smell enables them to follow their prey by collecting and analyzing the scent particles they have left behind.

One clear example is the Komodo monitor, or Komodo dragon, which lives on the islands of Indonesia and is up to 10 feet long. It attacks prey much larger than itself, such as horses and deer, but does not cause instant death because it is not poisonous. As the prey drags itself away mortally wounded, the monitor follows it and finds the corpse thanks to its sense of smell.

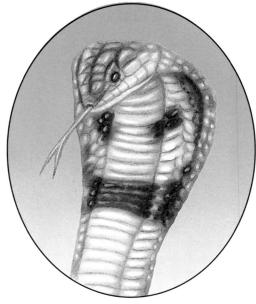

All snakes, even ones that are not poisonous, constantly stick out their tongues to collect information from all the scent particles they find.

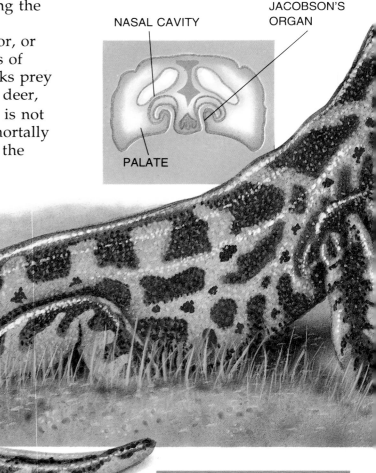

NASAL CAVITY

JACOBSON'S ORGAN

PALATE

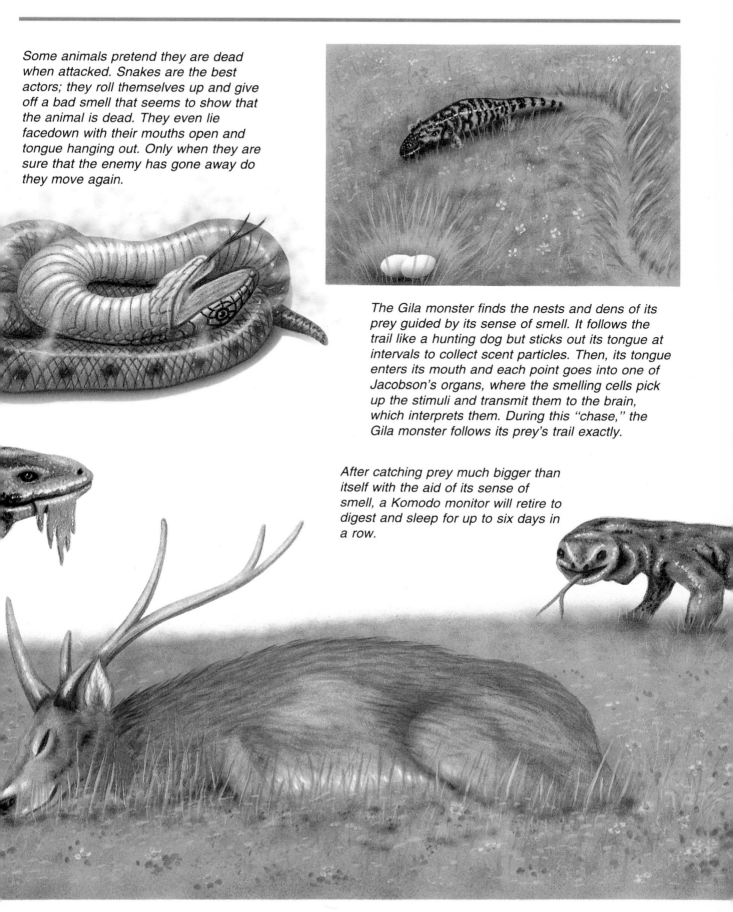

Some animals pretend they are dead when attacked. Snakes are the best actors; they roll themselves up and give off a bad smell that seems to show that the animal is dead. They even lie facedown with their mouths open and tongue hanging out. Only when they are sure that the enemy has gone away do they move again.

The Gila monster finds the nests and dens of its prey guided by its sense of smell. It follows the trail like a hunting dog but sticks out its tongue at intervals to collect scent particles. Then, its tongue enters its mouth and each point goes into one of Jacobson's organs, where the smelling cells pick up the stimuli and transmit them to the brain, which interprets them. During this "chase," the Gila monster follows its prey's trail exactly.

After catching prey much bigger than itself with the aid of its sense of smell, a Komodo monitor will retire to digest and sleep for up to six days in a row.

Mammal Scents

Of all vertebrates, mammals give most importance to smells.

Mammal skins have much influence in this feature, because they have sebaceous and sudoriferous glands that they have adapted to produce the complex smells they use to communicate.

The messages of smells can have many meanings, but they are most often used to mark possessions. Smell marks have the advantage of remaining long after they have been left and can dissuade intruders from entering occupied territory without a need for direct conflict.

Scientists believe that when mammals receive a smell message from another of the same species, they can "read" its sex, rank, age, reproductive state, and its diet, without even needing to see what animal left the smell.

Many mammals have several different odoriferous glands on their bodies and can send a different message with each. These glands are in different positions in different species. Elephants, for instance, have them behind their eyes; marmots have them in the middle of their loins; and capybaras have them on their snouts.

Marsupial babies, such as this red kangaroo, are not very developed when they are born and weigh less than 1 gram. To complete their development they must reach the marsupial bag and their mother's breast, guiding themselves only by their sense of smell.

One of the most highly developed senses of carnivores is smell, which not only serves as a means of communication but is also fundamental for looking for prey. Herbivores also need a very good sense of smell to detect their enemies.

At left you can see the violet gland, or supracaudal gland, which most canines have at the end of their tails. The function of this smelling gland is still a mystery.

Felines' smell is not usually as well developed as canines' smell.

The Search for Food

Each species has its own way of looking for food, and many have to search, sniff, and explore constantly to find some.

Many animals hunt under the darkness of night or inside caves, so they have a highly developed sense of smell. Hyenas, for instance, almost always go out at dusk to hunt, and during their hunt they may cover more than 62 miles (100 kilometers) in one dark night.

The sense of smell is very important for mammals from the time of birth. The young of many species cannot see or hear during the first few days of life, and they find their mother's breast through their sense of smell.

Herbivores do not have to hunt and attack to get food, but they use their smell to distinguish one plant from another.

Many insectivores have very developed "noses" and find their prey by means of their sense of smell, since insects are often well hidden. They can even smell them underground.

Vultures also use their sense of smell to find corpses to eat. They find them first using their sight, but then it is their smell that tells them if the animal is really dead.

The sense of smell is also important for feeding among social insects. For example, after eating, ants tell their companions where the food is by leaving a scent while returning to the nest.

The first thing that many animal mothers, such as this antelope, do is to eat their placental membranes and dry their newborn babies by licking them. In this way, they eliminate the smells that could attract predators.

During their migration each year in search of new pastures, gnus are guided by the smell of rain, which they can detect many miles away.

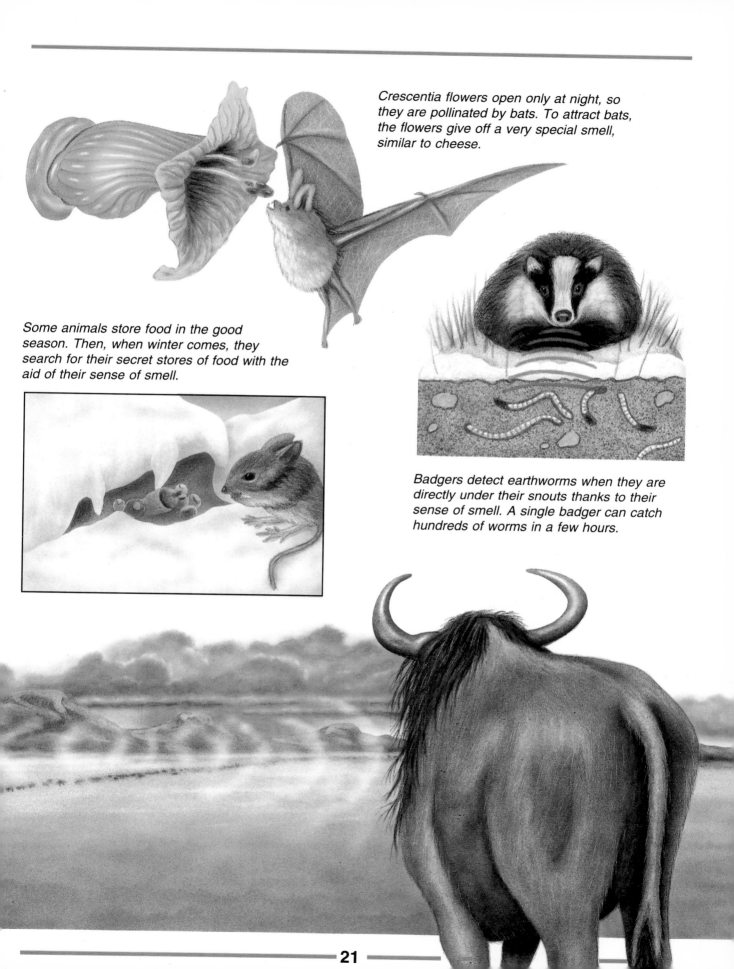

Crescentia flowers open only at night, so they are pollinated by bats. To attract bats, the flowers give off a very special smell, similar to cheese.

Some animals store food in the good season. Then, when winter comes, they search for their secret stores of food with the aid of their sense of smell.

Badgers detect earthworms when they are directly under their snouts thanks to their sense of smell. A single badger can catch hundreds of worms in a few hours.

Marking Territory

Most territorial species use smell marks to indicate their ownership of a certain area.

Many animals expel urine or feces as a normal way of marking specific points in their territory with their smell; other species rub special glands against objects. The owner regularly returns to the marked points, which are often the boundaries of its territory, and marks them again with its smell.

Smell marks on the perimeter of the space they defend can dissuade possible intruders without their presence. Thanks to the smell marks left behind, territory owners can see and follow all the movements of their rivals on the boundaries of their territory and avoid face-to-face confrontations. Tigers use urine mixed with anal secretions to mark brushwood, rocks, and trees. Neighboring tigers get to know each other well from the smells; males can sense the reproductive state of females and intruders are warned of the presence of the property owner.

Boundaries are broken and changed often, and each neighbor is aware of the movements of the others. Dominant members of wolf packs leave their smell marks on the boundaries of their territory so the members of the pack know where their territory ends to avoid entering the territories of other packs and causing conflicts that could be mortal.

Some animals, such as the cheetah or rhinoceros, mark their territory by urinating backward in a horizontal spray against a tree trunk or a rock.

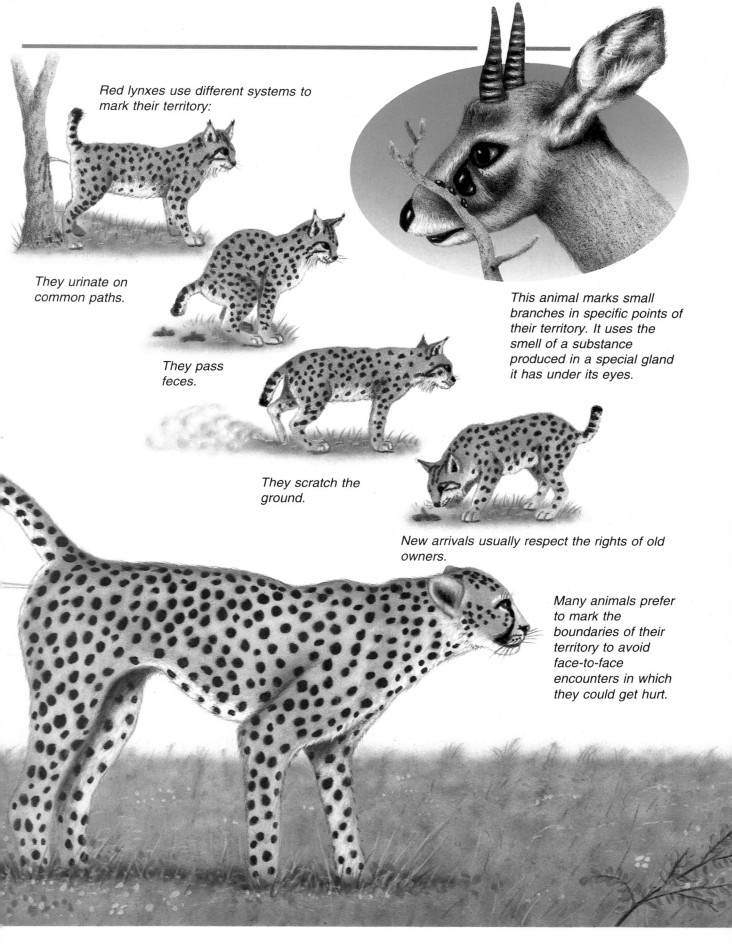

Red lynxes use different systems to mark their territory:

They urinate on common paths.

They pass feces.

They scratch the ground.

This animal marks small branches in specific points of their territory. It uses the smell of a substance produced in a special gland it has under its eyes.

New arrivals usually respect the rights of old owners.

Many animals prefer to mark the boundaries of their territory to avoid face-to-face encounters in which they could get hurt.

Love Messages

The sense of smell plays a very important role in reproduction.

Smell is one of the first senses that appeared in evolution. This is probably why it is so important in reproduction, from the initial attraction between members of different sexes to the recognition by mothers of their offspring.

When the time of year comes that females are ready to reproduce, they give off a chemical substance with a special smell. This substance can travel great distances in the air or water, and when males detect the ''love call'' they quickly use their sense of smell to go to the female.

When many male mammals detect the smell of a female in heat, they try to concentrate the smell entering the nasal cavities by raising their upper lips. They have a very typical expression that is not aggressive; the male has caught the fragrance in its nasal cavity to taste it, and it holds its breath with its upper lip forward and upward. By studying the smell, males know what state of receptiveness of the female is.

The smell glands only develop at the time of reproduction, and females cannot send these messages until they reach the reproductive age.

Sexual calls by smell are frequent among insects. This is why their antennae are highly developed, so that they can detect (like radar) all the smells in the air.

RHINOCEROUS

MOUNTAIN GOAT

The males of some mammal species lift their upper lips when they detect the smell of the love call of the females so they can intensify the sensation they receive.

Despite not having her in front of him, this tiger can find out a lot about the tigress that has left her smell mark. He can "read" her age, sex, maturity, and sexual receptiveness.

Lions sniff the lionesses to know whether they are in a receptive state for reproduction. The smell of the female informs the male of exactly the right moment.

Family Smells

There are many animals—particularly mammals—that can recognize one another thanks to their sense of smell.

The individual smells of babies enable mothers to recognize their own little ones from the rest. In the case of goats, for example, only a few minutes of smelling and licking is necessary for the mother to recognize her own kid. The scent is the most important sense during the first few days of a newborn's life, but as the baby grows, the mother can also recognize it by its voice or appearance. Mothers often eat the excrement of the babies during their first days to keep the den clean and get rid of all smells that could attract predators.

The babies of some other animals have developed a very special system to save themselves from predators. As well as hiding, their bodies do not smell during the first stages of their lives and so they cannot be detected by their predators' sensitive sense of smell.

Otters that live in groups use common *defecators*. There they mark a specific area, leaving it clear of vegetation and giving off a very strong smell of urine and feces secretions. The smell can be overpowering for days, if not weeks. Then, as the otters tread on the vegetation, they cover their fur with the smell the whole group spreads; they rub themselves on the ground and between each other until a smell is formed of the couple or the whole group.

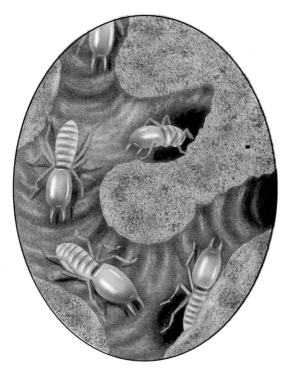

In termite colonies, the soldiers constantly produce a special pheromone. When there is too much concentration of the pheromone in the air it shows that there are too many soldiers in the termite nest. From then on, larvae are not allowed to become new soldiers until the ideal "soldier smell" level is retrieved.

A sea lion's sense of smell is so highly developed that females can recognize their cubs among thousands of others.

Bat mothers recognize their young among hundreds of others in the nursery by their particular smell. If the mothers do not find them, their children will die of hunger!

Here you can see how the members of a group of otters rub themselves against the surface where they have all left and mixed their feces and urine. They do this so they will all smell the same.

Odors of Defense

Most animals prefer to go unseen, but some emit striking odors to warn possible enemies of the risk they face if they attack.

One of the clearest examples of this is the skunk, which has an incredible weapon—it can give off a chemical substance with a lewd, irritating smell.

Any enemy hit by this discharge withdraws immediately, because not only is it nasty, but it also contains a substance that can be painful, especially for the sensitive snout of a predator (its delicate mucous membranes). If it catches the mouth, it can cause vomiting and terrible soreness, and temporary blindness in eyes. The liquid discharge can travel up to 10 feet. The smell is so strong it can be carried more than .62 miles by the wind.

Skunks always give warning before firing their fetid spray: they prefer not to waste their discharges because they cannot run the risk of being attacked by another predator until they have "recharged." They first pound the floor with their feet and arch their backs. If the enemy still insists despite this, they begin to swing their bodies and move 3 to 7 feet toward their enemy. To fire their discharge, skunks raise their tails, then they look over their enemy's shoulder, aim, and fire; while they fire they rock their body to cover a greater area with their spray and be sure of hitting the attacker.

Some small carnivores, such as foxes, mongooses, and ferrets, give off a repulsive smell when threatened, and this smell can put off their hungry enemies, which get the impression that the prey is not very appetizing.

STRIPED SKUNK   SPOTTED SKUNK

Not all skunks give the same warning signals. The striped skunk only raises its tail before releasing its foul spray, and the spotted skunk raises its hind legs and advances a few paces to make itself more visible.

Memories for smells enable them to be related to experiences that have happened. This fox is retreating because sometime in the past it had an unpleasant encounter with another skunk.

After receiving a direct discharge, any predator would immediately retreat, painfully rubbing its eyes and snout.

An Elephant's Trunk and Other Strange Noses

An elephant's trunk is the most famous nose in the animal kingdom.

It is strong and powerful, but it is also delicate. Despite being more than 7 feet (2 meters) long, a trunk is extraordinarily mobile due to its 40,000 groups of muscles. The end of African elephants' trunks is made up of two grasping appendages in the shape of a finger, which can be used very precisely. By contrast, Asian elephants only have one fingerlike appendage and their trunks are longer, smooth and ringless.

Trunks are almost smooth inside, but outside they are rounded and narrow toward the end. Inside a trunk there are very sensitive mucosas that are responsible for the fine sense of smell elephants have. These mucosas are also resistant to strange substances that elephants get in their trunks, such as dust and water.

Elephants, however, do not drink through their trunks. They actually fill their trunks with water—up to 2 gallons (9 liters)—and then put them in their mouths and release the water. Young elephants do not use their trunks to suckle, either.

When elephants smell the breeze in search of danger, they hold their trunks up. When they rest they roll them up or hang them on one of their tusks. To eat, elephants stretch out their trunks to branches as though they were arms and take the leaves to their mouths.

Although they usually defend themselves with their tusks, elephants can also use their trunks to hit their enemies.

Here is a strange primate with an enormous nose. Sometimes, males have such large noses that when they want to eat they have to lift their noses with their hands; females' noses are smaller but stand out more.

Camels can voluntarily open and close their nostrils. This is important for them to protect themselves against the sandstorms of the desert.

The small proboscis the saiga has on its cheek is due to the development of the nasal vestibule. This is a hollow chamber used to filter air breathed in, retain the dust, and heat cold air.

An elephant's trunk is the nose with most applications of all the animals; it can be used as an arm, hand, finger, lip, or nose.

INTERIOR TRUNK SECTION

Glossary

bifid separated into two equal lobes or parts by a median

cetacean aquatic marine animals, such as dolphins, whales, and porpoises, that have large heads, almost-hairless bodies, and paddle-shaped fore-limbs

cilia small hairs that cover some parts of the body of certain organisms

cuticle the resistant skin of arthropods; it covers part of the exterior of certain organisms, such as insects

defecator a place where excrement is deposited

larvae the first form of life that hatches

from the egg of amphibians and insects; it looks very different than it will as a mature adult

migration moving periodically from one region or climate to another for feeding or breeding

pheromones chemical substances that are produced by animals and serve as stimuli to other animals of the same species

proboscis a long flexible snout

spawn to produce eggs in aquatic animals that will result in numerous young

spiracle a breathing hole

Index